I0236317

IMAGES
of America

STAPLETON

Donated to the Staten Island Museum by the Mud Lane Society for the Renaissance of Stapleton, this hand-drawn aerial perspective dates from 1905. It is a photograph of one of two originals known to exist and was photographed by Ezzat F. El-Akkad. (Staten Island Museum Collection.)

ON THE COVER: The massive Bechtel Brewery, pictured at the height of its success, was located along Van Duzer Street at the top of Broad Street. (David Goldfarb collection.)

IMAGES
of America

STAPLETON

James G. Ferreri and David Goldfarb

ARCADIA
PUBLISHING

Copyright © 2010 by James G. Ferreri and David Goldfarb
ISBN 978-1-5316-4767-4

Published by Arcadia Publishing
Charleston SC, Chicago IL, Portsmouth NH, San Francisco
CA

Library of Congress Control Number: 2009936186

For all general information contact Arcadia Publishing at:
Telephone 843-853-2070
Fax 843-853-0044
E-mail sales@arcadiapublishing.com
For customer service and orders:
Toll-Free 1-888-313-2665

Visit us on the Internet at www.arcadiapublishing.com

CONTENTS

ACKNOWLEDGMENTS

The authors would like to thank the following individuals and organizations for their help in assembling many of the photographs used in this book: Elizabeth Egbert, president and CEO of the Staten Island Museum, for her generosity in opening the archives to us; Cara Dellate, assistant archivist at the Staten Island Museum, for her time in assembling our selection of photographs from the museum that appear herein; and Patricia Salmon, Staten Island Museum's curator of history, for her patience. Each time she was asked for information about the town of Stapleton, a subject near and dear to her, she was quick to respond to any inquiry. The authors would also like to thank Marjorie Decker Johnson for her support in checking dates and Dr. W. Ted Brown for permission to use images from his personal collection. Thanks also go to Catherine "Mac" O'Callaghan for granting permission to use photographs of her house and the events that took place there. Special thanks, also, to Danny Blaine, great-nephew of the founder of the Stapleton "Stapes," for allowing us to use the images from the testimonial honoring his late relative. We would also like to thank scholar and historian Barnett Shepard for his assistance, especially regarding the Ward House and the Boardman-Mitchell House.

We would also like to acknowledge the efforts of the Mud Lane Society for the Renaissance of Stapleton, the Preservation League of Staten Island, and the Historic Districts Council of New York City for their efforts in obtaining a New York City Landmarks Designation for the St. Paul's Avenue-Stapleton Heights Historic District.

In particular, we would like to acknowledge the work of Cynthia Mailman and W. Ted Brown as past presidents of the Mud Lane Society for their efforts.

Jim Ferreri would like to personally thank Patricia Salmon for her aid. Pat never refused to assist in finding a requested tidbit of necessary information on the many occasions such information was requested. Her friendship and council are truly appreciated.

David Goldfarb would like to thank his wife, Elizabeth K. Goldfarb, for her patience and support while he worked on this book.

INTRODUCTION

The Aquehonga Indians, a branch of the Raritans, were the first inhabitants of Staten Island's shoreline, where they capitalized on the abundance of food available from the surrounding waterways. Giovanni da Verrazzano first discovered Staten Island in 1524 while looking for a route to the East Indies. In 1609, Henry Hudson, attempting for the third time to find a route to the Orient, anchored off "Staaten Eylandt." The first Dutch settlements were at South Beach and the "Watering Place" in Tompkinsville but certainly the Dutch also explored the area known today as Stapleton. During the 18th century, the English took possession from the Dutch, and Staten Island was to be a Tory stronghold during the Revolutionary War; the British troops finally left the island in 1783.

During the 19th century, Stapleton was known as the most important village on Staten Island's eastern shore. This village owes its existence as much to the Tompkins family as does nearby Tompkinsville, both having been built on land that was owned by that family.

Founder of Tompkinsville and former vice president Daniel D. Tompkins died in 1825. Prior to his death, his landholdings were lost to insolvency, and his nephew, Caleb T. Ward, bought some of these parcels. Ward had moved to Staten Island around 1818 to begin working at several different posts in his uncle's business ventures. Caleb Ward later served as one of the trustees responsible for liquidating his late uncle's assets, as well as being coexecutor of the will, along with his aunt, Mrs. D. D. Tompkins.

By 1827, Ward built himself a house near Tompkinsville, and by 1829, he hired a surveyor to lay out the portions of his holdings north of Tompkinsville into streets and lots. Richmond Street, today's St. Paul's Avenue, formed the spine of this planned development area. By this time, Ward had already sold some lots, and a few houses were now standing; the largest being the home of his cousin, Griffen Tompkins, which still stands at 138 St. Paul's Avenue.

In 1833, Caleb T. Ward donated several lots along Richmond Street (St. Paul's Avenue) to the newly formed Protestant Episcopal congregation of Tompkinsville, realizing the importance a church would have in the sales and development of his lots. By 1835, a Greek Revival wood-frame church building was standing at the spot of today's 164 St. Paul's Avenue, and it remained in use until 1870, at which time it was demolished. The original rectory for this building still stands at 172 St. Paul's Avenue as a private home.

Around the same time as the Ward donation to the Episcopal parish, New York City merchant William J. Staples and his partner, Minthorne Tompkins, son of Daniel D. Tompkins, purchased a large tract of land from the Vanderbilt clan on Staten Island's east shore, near the foot of present-day Broad Street. Staples and Tompkins had the lands laid out into streets and lots, opting to use Staples's last name for their venture, since the Tompkins name was already used with the founding of Tompkinsville; thus, in 1836, Stapleton came into being.

In 1837, the Seaman's Retreat and Hospital was operating nearby in an imposing Greek Revival building. The hospital was founded to care for sick and disabled merchant sailors on a sprawling 40-acre site at Bay Street and Vanderbilt Avenue.

In order to more easily sell their building lots, Staples and Tompkins founded ferry service to Manhattan and subsequently began advertising their new development. As a result of the ferry service, and the development of rail service, Stapleton grew rapidly. With this rapid growth came jobs, and with jobs the demand for housing increased.

Besides the stunning views from its hilly terrain, Stapleton was blessed with an abundance of natural resources, such as artesian springs and ancient and cool caverns and caves that attracted brewery founders to the area. The largest, as well as one of the earliest, to settle in Stapleton was the Bechtel Brewery on Van Duzer Street at the top of Broad Street, founded in 1853. Soon additional breweries were established alongside other large German-owned businesses, with the result that Stapleton was to become one of the major German enclaves in New York, as well as in the entire northeastern United States.

Prior to the Civil War there were many picturesque homes built in the reigning architectural styles then being popularized by Samuel Sloan, Calvert Vaux, and Andrew Jackson Downing; styles such as the Italianate villa style and the Gothic Revival cottage took their places alongside the earlier Greek Revival buildings in the area. The sloping hills of Stapleton were the perfect setting for the romantic architecture then in vogue, making the area one of the more sought after and picturesque in New York.

The years during the Civil War saw industry flourish on Staten Island, and the Stapleton shipyards and piers became leading locations for commerce with military vessels and commercial ships.

The decades following the war saw the Bechtel Brewery prosper, making the founder's son, George Bechtel, Staten Island's largest taxpayer. Bechtel built a massive home for himself, which has been lost, as well as the stunning Queen Anne home he commissioned for his daughter as a wedding gift that still stands at 387 St. Paul's Avenue. This turreted gem is considered by many to be the best example of the Queen Anne, wood-frame home still standing in New York City.

Stapleton was also the home of the Stapleton "Stapes," an early NFL franchise that played at Thompson Stadium, which is the site of the Stapleton Houses housing project today. The addition of a low income project to the main business section of the village, combined with the move away from downtown shopping areas, caused a slide in Stapleton's fortunes that continued for much of the second half of the 20th century.

Today, thanks to the designation of the St. Paul's Avenue-Stapleton Heights Historic District, many of the dazzling and imposing homes along St. Paul's Avenue and the surrounding streets are protected from ill-advised development. There has been a resurgence of interest in the area, both by businesses and home owners, due to Stapleton's proximity to Manhattan and the Verrazano-Narrows Bridge; so much so, that the Stapleton of today shows a real vitality once again.

One

EARLY SETTLEMENT

Staten Island of the early 19th century was a community whose economy continued to be, as it had always been, tied to its surrounding waterways.

As happened throughout recorded history, the waterfront was the location where early settlers made their homes. Native Americans inhabited the shoreline regions to capitalize on the abundance of food available from the seas and lakes, as well as the fact that their transportation from site to site was made possible via small boats on the water, facilitating further settlement to occur.

The first Dutch settlers in New Amsterdam founded their communities at the tip of Manhattan Island, and Staten Island's first settlement was at a point near today's South Beach.

The lands on which the village of Stapleton was founded boasted a shore location that included land ascending up the steep and hilly terrain that had originally been part of the Vanderbilt family holdings. The fact that Stapleton was in such close proximity to navigable waters would play an important part in its development.

William J. Staples, a New York City merchant, and Minthorne Tompkins, son of former vice president Daniel D. Tompkins, purchased a large portion of the Vanderbilt's holdings and founded the village as a business enterprise in the early 1830s, naming their venture "Stapleton" in 1836. The central artery of the village was Broad Street, which connected the shore with the more inland portions of the community. Shortly after Tompkins and Staples had lots laid out and roads mapped, the partners founded ferry service from the foot of Broad Street to Manhattan Island and began advertising the settlement in order to sell their lots.

With the success of their venture came an increase in population along with the influx of businesses to the area; Stapleton began to flourish, and over the next 20 years, due in no small measure to its excellent port with its steam ferry service, Stapleton grew rapidly, quickly becoming the most important village on Staten Island's east shore.

This mural depicts a Native American settlement on Staten Island. When discovered by Europeans, the Aquehonga Indians, a branch of the Raritans, occupied Staten Island. There are several Native American burial grounds while numerous Indian relics have been found across Staten Island. This Works Progress Administration (WPA) mural from Staten Island Borough Hall is by Frederick Charles Stahr. (David Goldfarb collection.)

Frederick Charles Stahr was born in 1876. He studied at the National Academy of Design and became an instructor at Columbia University. In 1904, Stahr proposed painting murals of the history of Staten Island in the new borough hall. He was promised the commission, but due to insufficient funds, the murals were not painted until the WPA awarded the commission 32 years later. (David Goldfarb collection.)

Giovanni da Verrazzano (1485–1528)
discovered Staten Island in 1524 while
searching for a route to the East Indies.
Verrazzano was an Italian explorer
in service to the French crown. He is
renowned as the first European since
the Norse to explore the Atlantic coast
of North America. This mural from the
Staten Island Borough Hall is by Frederick
Charles Stahr. (David Goldfarb collection.)

In 1609, Henry Hudson, attempting for the
third time to find a route to the Orient,
is anchored off "Staaten Eylandt" while
Native Americans stand on the shore.
This mural is from the Staten Island
Borough Hall and is by Frederick Charles
Stahr. (David Goldfarb collection.)

11

In 1630, the Dutch West India Company granted Staten Island to Michael Pauw as a part of his patroonship of Pavonia (Bayonne, Jersey City, and Hoboken). It was bought at this time from the Native Americans for "some duffels, kettles, axes, hoes, wampum, drilling awls, 'Jew's' harps, and other small wares." Before Pauw had established a settlement, he sold it back to the Dutch West India Company. There were four Staten Island patroons of which Michael Pauw was the first. His patroonship included all of Staten Island and parts of New Jersey. In 1636, David De Vries took over Pauw's patroonship. De Vries landed at the "Watering Place" (today's Tompkinsville), to build Staten Island's first colony in 1639. This WPA mural from the Staten Island Borough Hall is by Frederick Charles Stahr. (David Goldfarb collection.)

This Frederick Stahr WPA mural depicts Cornelis Melyn trading with the Native Americans. Cornelius Melyn became the third patroon in June 1642, at which time De Vries agreed to give him Staten Island, with the exception of the De Vries plantation. Native Americans destroyed Melyn's settlement during the "Whiskey War," and Melyn fled to New Amsterdam. In 1650, Melyn returned to Staten Island and again built farms. Melyn's colony was once again destroyed by the Native Americans, and he left Staten Island, returning to Holland. (David Goldfarb collection.)

This Frederick Stahr WPA mural depicts the British troops evacuating Staten Island on December 5, 1783. The Treaty of Paris, which ended the Revolutionary War, stated that the British would withdraw their garrison and fleets from the United States. (David Goldfarb collection.)

Pictured is the Bay of New York as viewed from the Narrows in this print by W. Pate. (David Goldfarb collection.)

The Narrows, as seen from Pavilion Hill in Tompkinsville, shows the Stapleton shoreline curving away toward the center of the image, while the Caleb T. Ward Mansion is seen at the extreme right. The image was found in the book *Staaten Island,* published by Herman J. Meyer (Meyer's Universum, 1859). (David Goldfarb collection.)

This c. 1861 painting shows Stapleton across the Narrows, as seen from Fort Hamilton in Brooklyn. Stapleton is located along the hilly terrain to the right and behind the small pavilion set in the water near the center of the image. Note the many tall-masted ships visible along the Stapleton shore. The original painting was by Frances Flora Bond Palmer. (Staten Island Museum Collection.)

This early sketch of the Vanderbilt home in Stapleton is mislabeled as the birthplace of Cornelius Vanderbilt. Vanderbilt was born in Port Richmond in 1794 and moved with his family to Stapleton as a young boy. (Staten Island Museum Collection.)

Commodore Cornelius Vanderbilt operated a flat boat named *Dread* from Staten Island to New York City by 1812. By 1817, Vanderbilt was running a steam ferry service between New York and New Brunswick, New Jersey, where he lived until 1829, returning to Staten Island that same year. Cornelius Vanderbilt was Staten Island's first millionaire. This daguerreotype attributed to Matthew Brady shows "the Commodore" later in his life. (Library of Congress.)

These two images show the Stapleton home that Cornelius Vanderbilt grew up in. Using $100 that he borrowed from his mother to buy his first small boat, it was from this house that he started his ferry service to New York City at age 17. (Above, David Goldfarb collection; below, Staten Island Museum Collection.)

These two sketches show the Van Duzer homestead. The Van Duzer family was the immediate neighbor to the Vanderbilts in Stapleton. Early ferry service from Stapleton was actually run by Abraham Van Duzer, between this section of Staten Island and New York City (Manhattan). Today's Richmond Road was originally named for the Van Duzer family. The road ran from Van Duzer's Ferry (Stapleton) to Richmond Town, and this section still retains the Van Duzer name. (Both, Staten Island Museum Collection.)

Vanduzer Homestead, Stapleton.

Two

SCENIC STAPLETON

Stapleton's topography is in no small way responsible for its natural beauty; that of hills sloping to the shore.

By the 1870s, the east shore villages of Tompkinsville, Stapleton, and Clifton were consolidated into the incorporated Village of Edgewater. All three shared this graceful topographical aspect of hills and shoreline, creating a most desirable location in which to live and work. The area seemed custom made for the picturesque architecture then in vogue throughout the country.

Due to the fact that Stapleton was the area's transportation hub, as well as the political center of Edgewater, it grew at a rapid pace. As the inhabitants prospered, homes became larger and more elaborate, while the winding and/or sloping residential streets became the most sought after addresses in the area to live.

With its two major churches and elaborate mansions, St. Paul's Avenue would become one of the most scenic streets on Staten Island. Broad Street, with its steep slope up from the shore, became one of the major business thoroughfares in Edgewater, while the streets surrounding the town square, then known as Washington Square, would support many small businesses well into the 20th century.

When originally built, Washington Square had water views from all vantage points in the park. The Edgewater Village Hall was located within this public area, and there was ample room to stroll and relax along the curving walkways under spreading trees.

Photographs taken of Stapleton in the third quarter of the 19th century show an array of lovely homes on tree-lined streets. The beauty of these Victorian-era streetscapes seems to capture all the romance and splendor that people, both consciously and unconsciously, attribute to the Gilded Age in America; that of houses with awnings shading large front porches in summer or of children sledding down a sloping terrain in winter.

Most of the homes built on the hillsides had harbor views, and from these vantage points, those lucky homeowners would be able to watch the parade of tall ships passing through the Narrows on their way into New York Harbor from ports the world over.

This stereoscopic view is labeled "View of Stapleton Heights, Staten Island" and is from *Anthony's Stereoscopic Views No. 5432*, published by E. and H. T. Anthony and Company. The image shows Stapleton from the heights right down to the waterfront. The large building to the left with the mansard-roofed tower is the R and H Brewery. (David Goldfarb collection.)

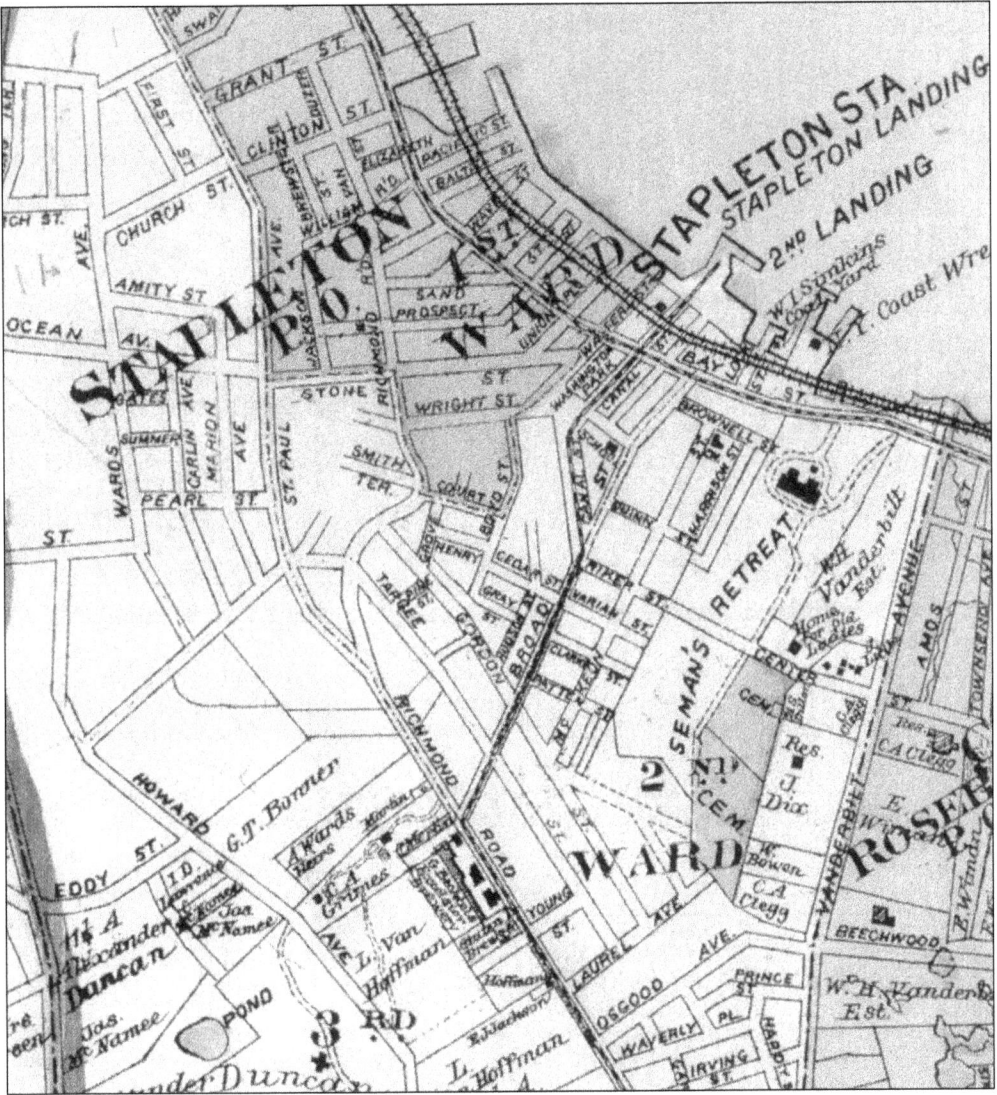

This is Beer's Atlas, dated 1887, showing late-19th-century Stapleton. Note the large parcel to the right near the waterfront labeled Vanderbilt Estate. Also notice that the "Home for Old Ladies" was in existence at this time. By the period of this atlas, the shoreline has been extended, allowing for the construction of train tracks for the Staten Island Railroad. Also toward the center of the image, one can discern that the town square is still named Washington Park. Note that Van Duzer Street, as it is known today, was at the time named Richmond Road. (Staten Island Museum Collection.)

Isaac Almstaedt, photographic chronicler of Staten Island in the late 19th and early 20th centuries and considered a master at his scenic shots, took the above photograph from Stapleton Heights, known today as Grymes Hill. As Stapleton grew, it grew as most waterfront communities did throughout history, first near the shore, and then inland, as the photograph shows, the community has achieved quite a degree of denseness. The large building to the right with the mansard-roofed tower is the R and H Brewery. Below is another view from the hills above Stapleton. (Both, Staten Island Museum Collection.)

View from the Hills above Stapleton.   Staten Island, N. Y.

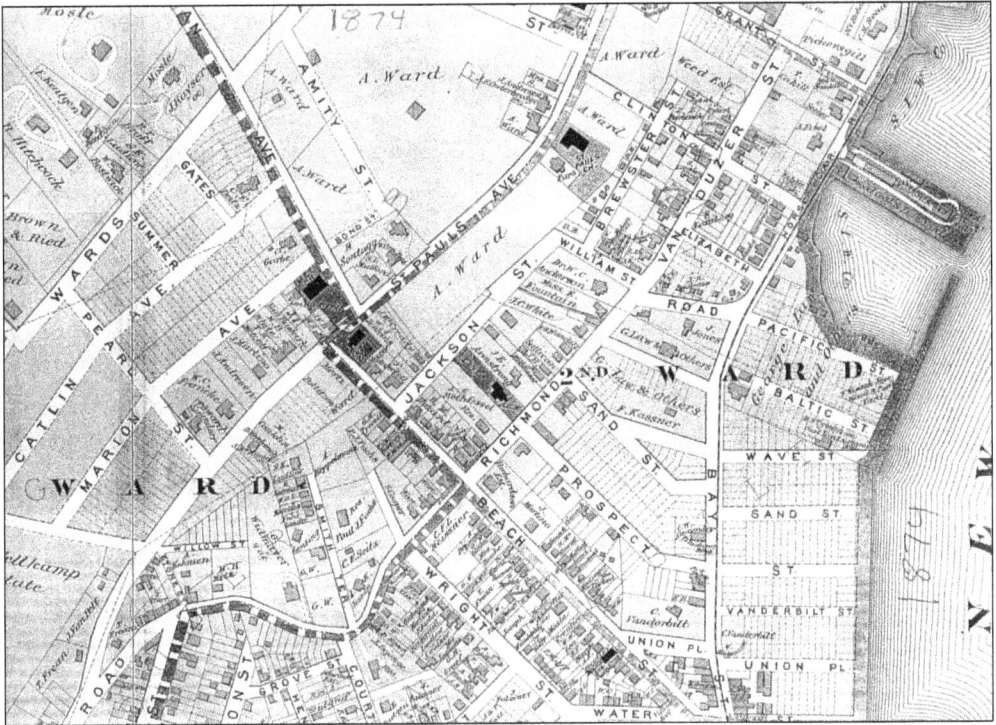

An atlas of Stapleton dated 1874 clearly shows that the Vanderbilts are still represented in the area in the large parcel at the bottom of the image, just right of center. (Dr. W. Ted Brown collection.)

The "Hills of Stapleton from the N.Y. Bay" is an early photograph that shows the mansions that once lined the cliffs of Grymes Hill, with a clear view of the Greek Revival Ward Mansion to the right of the photograph. Note the busy docks along the Stapleton waterfront. (Staten Island Museum Collection.)

The image above is a wide view of Van Duzer Street in Stapleton dated 1921. The image below of Richmond Road near Van Duzer Street shows earlier and smaller homes built before the roads were paved and widened; many have makeshift stoops or none at all. The ubiquitous Roulston stores are represented by the small grocery at the corner in the foreground of the photograph. (Staten Island Museum Collection.)

Beautiful Beach Street (note the misspelling), as it appeared early in the 20th century, is a far cry from today's mix of commercial and residential structures. (Staten Island Museum Collection.)

This is another image of Beach Street; this time from around 1927. The double house at the center of the photograph lasted, in derelict form, into the 21st century but was sadly recently demolished. (Staten Island Museum Collection.)

An Isaac Almstaedt photograph of Stapleton, above, appears to show the intersection of Bay and Broad Streets. The caption on the back of the photograph reads, "View from Tynans Building, Stapleton." The same view many decades later, below, shows that the image was indeed of Bay and Broad Streets. The caption on the rear of this photograph reads, "V. Ames, View from Edgewater Hall, Stapleton." The building in the center of the photograph, built parallel to Broad Street, is the home of the Salvation Army. Note that all of the empty lots that appeared in the earlier Almstaedt photograph have been filled. There is a *c.* 1980 Cadillac Seville parked perpendicular to the curb on Broad Street, so the photograph can be dated as late 20th century. (Staten Island Museum Collection.)

This is Grove Street as it appeared in 1927. Small early-19th-century homes in the foreground are knit closely together, while the grander homes further up the hills take in the sweeping vistas that this part of Staten Island afforded due to its unique topography. (Staten Island Museum Collection.)

This c. 1934 image, taken from Grove Street looking up to the crest of Grymes Hill (Stapleton Heights), clearly shows the prominence of Hormann Castle. Note the many winding roads and the delivery truck at center, which is wending its way toward the camera. (Staten Island Museum Collection.)

In this early postcard view, a horse and buggy shares Bay Street with a trolley. The view is from the town square. (David Goldfarb collection.)

An early-20th-century image taken of Bay Street looking north toward Canal Street in the distance shows a horse and buggy parked on the east side of the cobblestone paved street, while a trolley wends its way toward the camera. (Staten Island Museum Collection.)

Bird's Eye View, St. Pauls Ave., Stapleton, S. I.

The image above reveals St. Paul's Avenue early in its history. Young trees have been planted along the road in front of the grand homes built on the crest of the hill. During the 1840s, St. Paul's Avenue was named "Mud Lane" in honor of its unpaved status at the time. Before the street was paved and sewers installed, heavy rains would wash down the hillside onto the thoroughfare, thus, "Mud Lane." The image below is an 1898 map of Stapleton showing St. Paul's Avenue. (Above, Staten Island Museum Collection; below, Dr. W. Ted Brown collection.)

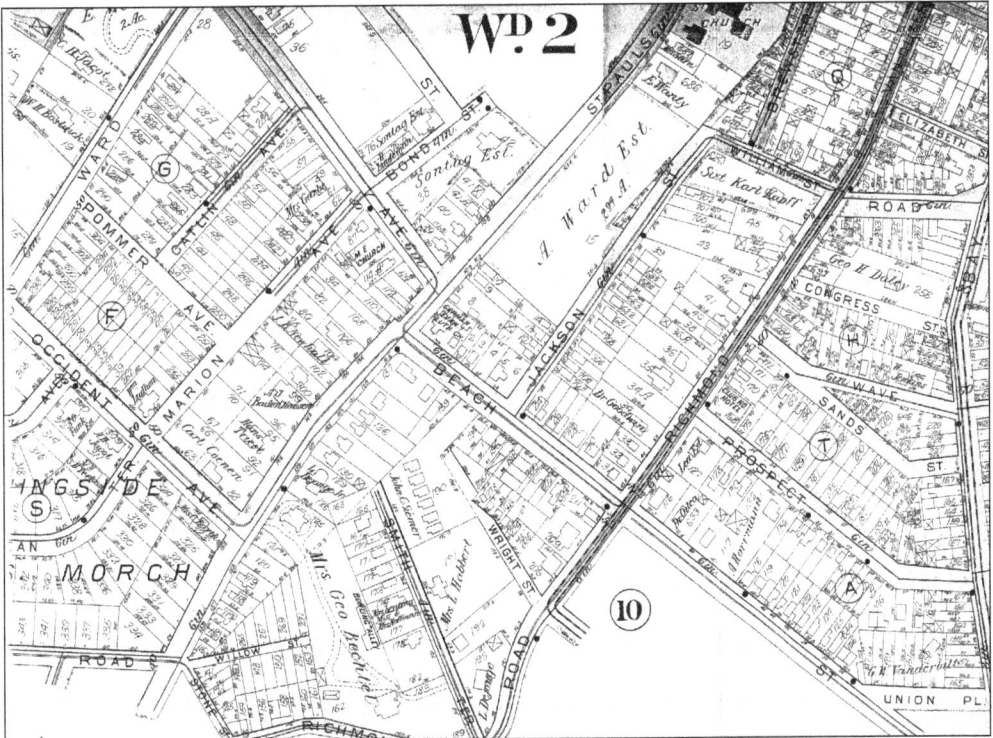

Here is a beautiful summertime view of Wright Street at Van Duzer Street; note the trolley heading toward the camera. (Dr. W. Ted Brown collection.)

This is the intersection of Van Duzer and Beach Streets. This photograph was taken at the time that straw hats in summer were a must for the well-dressed Staten Island gentleman. The building to the right is still standing, but across Beach Street, the block today is unrecognizable. (Staten Island Museum Collection.)

May Christmas bring you joy.

Washington Park, Stapleton, S. I.

Washington Square (today's Tappen Park) is the image chosen for this Christmas card, or was it possibly an advertisement for the shopping center surrounding the park? It does seem ironic that the image shows the town square in summer. Note the knickers on the boy and the full bustle of the Victorian dress. (Staten Island Museum Collection.)

"The Old Town Square" is the title of this summertime view of Stapleton. Note the trolley and the auto, which places this photograph somewhere around 1915 to 1920. (Staten Island Museum Collection.)

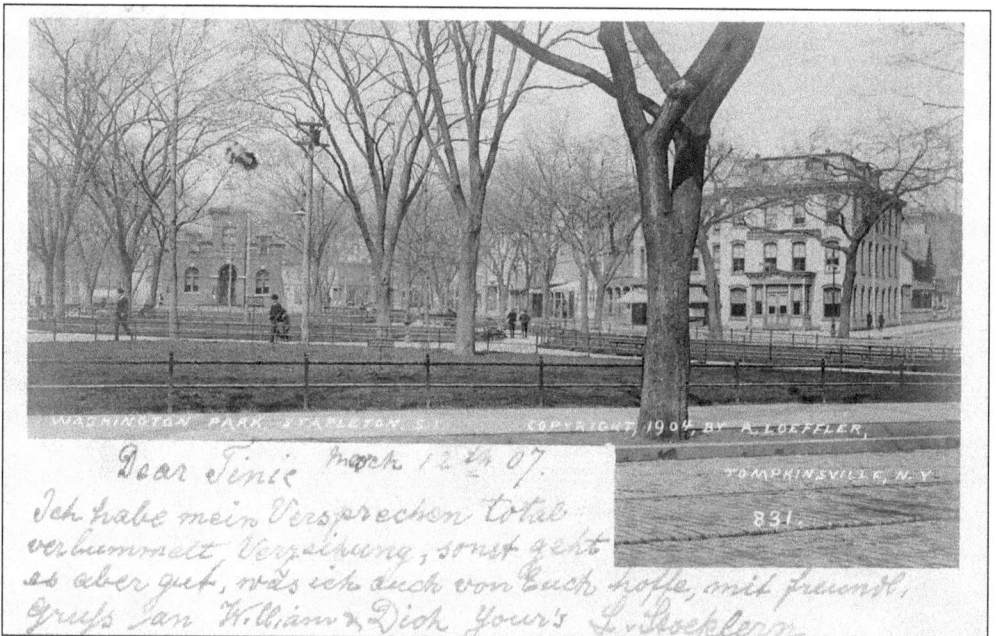

Staten Island Savings Bank is seen through the trees in Washington Park, an early name for today's Tappen Park. This postcard image from 1904 illustrates how graceful and civilized Stapleton's town center was at the start of the 20th century. The village hall is visible to the left of the image. The inscription is dated 1907, and, as appropriate to the large German populace in Stapleton, is written in that language. (Staten Island Museum Collection.)

Water St. & Public Park, Stapleton, Staten Island, N. Y.

Victorian Stapleton with all its finery is on display on Water Street. The park is across from the large building to the left, on whose large window is painted Department of Health, while the storefront adjacent sells coffees and teas, long before any Starbucks chain stores existed. Note the horse and buggy parked on the "wrong" side of the road. (Staten Island Museum Collection.)

Business Section, Stapleton
Staten Island, N. Y.

The same street scene a few decades into the future shows that Woolworth's five-and-dime store now occupies the building that housed the Department of Health. The national shoe store chains, Miles and Thom McCann Shoes, have a presence in the shopping district right next door. This summer scene shows 1940s-era Staten Islanders enjoying Tappen Park as they shop and work. (Staten Island Museum Collection.)

This is a view of Washington Park from the village hall toward Bay Street, taken around 1923. Note the iron fencing that remains even today. The redbrick building with the cement columns is currently a branch of the Chase bank. (David Goldfarb collection.)

A c. 1961 view of Tappen Park, looking toward Staten Island Savings Bank, shows a 100-plus-year-old horse chestnut tree that today is listed as one of the "great trees of Staten Island." (Staten Island Museum Collection.)

This is maritime Stapleton in its prime. The Stapleton Ferry terminal, long before the train system arrived along the shore, has horses pulling wagons loaded with produce and supplies that await the ferry, while a tall-masted ship passes close by. (Staten Island Museum Collection.)

This early-20th-century image of the *Stapleton* shows that the designs for the ferryboats plying New York Harbor have changed little over the last century. Today's modern ferries, although consisting of three decks, remarkably resemble the basic shape of the older boats, with the exception that they no longer can transport automobiles on their lower level. (Staten Island Museum Collection.)

This photograph by famous Staten Island woman photographer Alice Austen depicts warships (Dewey's White Fleet) from the slope of Grymes Hill. It was taken at 3:15 p.m. on Wednesday, April 20, 1897. (Dr. W. Ted Brown collection.)

A noticeably low-rise Manhattan is seen from the Stapleton shore. Early modes of maritime transportation, all with sails, form a parade past both shorelines. (Staten Island Museum Collection.)

New York Bay, from the Marine Hospital in Stapleton, clearly shows the shoreline before landfill was brought in to widen the shore for the Staten Island Rapid Transit Line tracks to be installed. The beautiful view from the Marine Hospital of the Narrows makes it quite clear why a facility for maritime patients would have been built at this location. (Staten Island Museum Collection.)

Staten Island's, as well as Stapleton's, maritime history is on full display in this *c.* 1905 postcard view. At the crest of the hill, near the left mast of the large ship, is the Greek Revival Ward Mansion. (Staten Island Museum Collection.)

U.S. transports *McClellan* and *Kirkpatrick* are shown at Brady's Pier. The USS *Kirkpatrick* was a destroyer escort built for the navy and launched in 1943. U.S. Army transport *McClellan* was purchased by the army in 1898 and used as a troop ship until converted into a refrigerator ship, where fresh meat for the army could be stored and frozen before going to the battle front. This photograph is by J. K. Dehler. (David Goldfarb collection.)

This postcard view of the Stapleton Harbor shows the variety of ships that were moored there, including transports, fishing boats, tugboats, small sailboats, and tall ships. (David Goldfarb collection.)

Stapleton and the new Piers   Staten Island, N. Y.

New York City built piers in Stapleton around 1920. From 1937 to 1942, several were used as the first foreign trade zone in the United States. During World War II, these piers became the New York Port of Embarkation for the U.S. Army. After the war, the piers again became a foreign trade zone. As their use declined, most were demolished by the 1970s. (David Goldfarb collection.)

A view looking over Stapleton shows the R and H Brewery visible at the extreme left of the photograph. The brewery's two smokestacks, as well as its convex-shaped mansard-roofed tower, were island landmarks for decades. (Staten Island Museum Collection.)

This is a splendid postcard view taken from the Hormann Castle grounds on Howard Avenue, looking toward the Narrows with Stapleton clearly visible to the shoreline below. Brooklyn is visible across the Narrows, which is filled with large sailing vessels on this particular day. Note that the view is minus the Verrazano-Narrows Bridge, which opened to traffic in 1964, connecting Brooklyn and Staten Island. (Staten Island Museum Collection.)

In this view of Stapleton, dated November 1934, one can see how populated the town has become and how important Stapleton's shoreline was to the community's economic stability. The many piers represented hundreds of jobs and a good deal of income. Notice that Brooklyn's shore, where today one drives the Belt Parkway, was remarkably undeveloped at this time. (Staten Island Museum Collection.)

This lovely c. 1900 view of Stapleton was taken from Serpentine Road, which was an early name for Howard Avenue. Many of the grand homes that were built late in the 19th century along St. Paul's Avenue are clearly visible at the center of the photograph. (Staten Island Museum Collection.)

A View of Stapleton S. I.

This postcard view of Stapleton from around 1910 shows the variety of houses, rooflines, porches, and window styles that were present. Also note the large amount of remaining undeveloped space. (Dr. W. Ted Brown collection.)

A 25586   St. Paul's Ave. and Morningside, Stapleton, N. Y.

This view of St. Paul's Avenue and Morningside Avenue shows some of the same houses as in the postcard view above. Note that the same house and porch in the left foreground can be seen in both images. Some of the area's larger homes, as well as Ward Mansion, can be seen in the background. (Staten Island Museum Collection.)

Three

EARLY RESIDENTIAL ARCHITECTURE

Most Americans will answer in the affirmative when asked if they have heard of the Vanderbilt name. However, how many realize that the man who would amass one of the greatest American fortunes of the 19th century, Commodore Cornelius Vanderbilt, was born and raised right here on Staten Island is another matter altogether.

Although he was born elsewhere on Staten Island, Vanderbilt was reared from an early age in Stapleton. One can deduce from this fact, then, that Stapleton was always a choice residential location among 18th-and-19th-century Staten Islanders, since the Vanderbilt clan had large land holdings by the early 19th century and could choose to live anywhere. The Commodore's boyhood home in Stapleton was built in the Dutch Colonial style, then so prevalent on the island, and stood to the rear of where the Paramount Theater on Bay Street stands today.

There were many homes built in the early 19th century in Stapleton that still stand, such as the home at the corner of Broad and Van Duzer Streets. The oldest portion of this building dates to around 1830 and appears on maps as early as the 1840s. The building grew in stages, and today one can discern three separate building styles that connect to form a long and quite historical whole. It was owned at one time by Theodore Frean, a lawyer who would eventually own many parcels around the entire Stapleton area. The next style of home to appear in Stapleton was the Greek Revival, and many of these c. 1840 homes still stand. Sadly though, the massive Greek Revival home built by the Vanderbilt family adjacent to the smaller family homestead has been lost.

This is the massive *c.* 1835 Greek Revival–style home of the Vanderbilt clan as it appeared early in the 20th century. The home, obviously, was built to represent the family's changing status from that of country farmers to one of prestige and influence. The home stood with its front along Bay Street and essentially to the rear of today's Paramount Theater. At the time that this photograph was taken, the lot is seriously overgrown and the once stately home is in obvious disrepair. (Staten Island Museum Collection.)

One of the scores and scores of Greek Revival gems still standing on Staten Island, this example is on Van Duzer Street. Notice the "springing eve" detail at the front of the roofline. This curving roof detail was prominent in many cities in the northeastern United States and hearkens back to the early Dutch houses in New Netherlands. (Staten Island Museum Collection.)

This is the Caleb T. Ward Mansion, as photographed around 1910. The mansion was the focal point of Ward's 250-acre estate. In 1826, Ward purchased property at the pinnacle of the hill that would bear his name, and in 1835, he hired Seth Geer to design his Greek Revival–style home. The site that Ward chose for the home capitalized on the panoramic views of Staten Island, New York Harbor, and the Narrows. The house remained in the Ward family until 1904 when it was purchased by Lewis and Sally Wood Nixon from the heirs. Lewis Nixon was an acclaimed naval designer and commissioner of public works for the Borough of Richmond from 1914 to 1915. Nixon Avenue, which surrounds the mansion today by hugging the crest of the hill, was laid out in the 1920s. (Staten Island Museum Collection.)

Built on the corner of the large Ward family lot around 1845, this elegant Italianate home at 218 St. Paul's Avenue directly faces St. Paul's Church. It was built by Albert Ward as an investment property, and in his dotage, he lived in it. When he was too infirm to attend mass, the church doors were left open so that he could participate. (James G. Ferreri collection.)

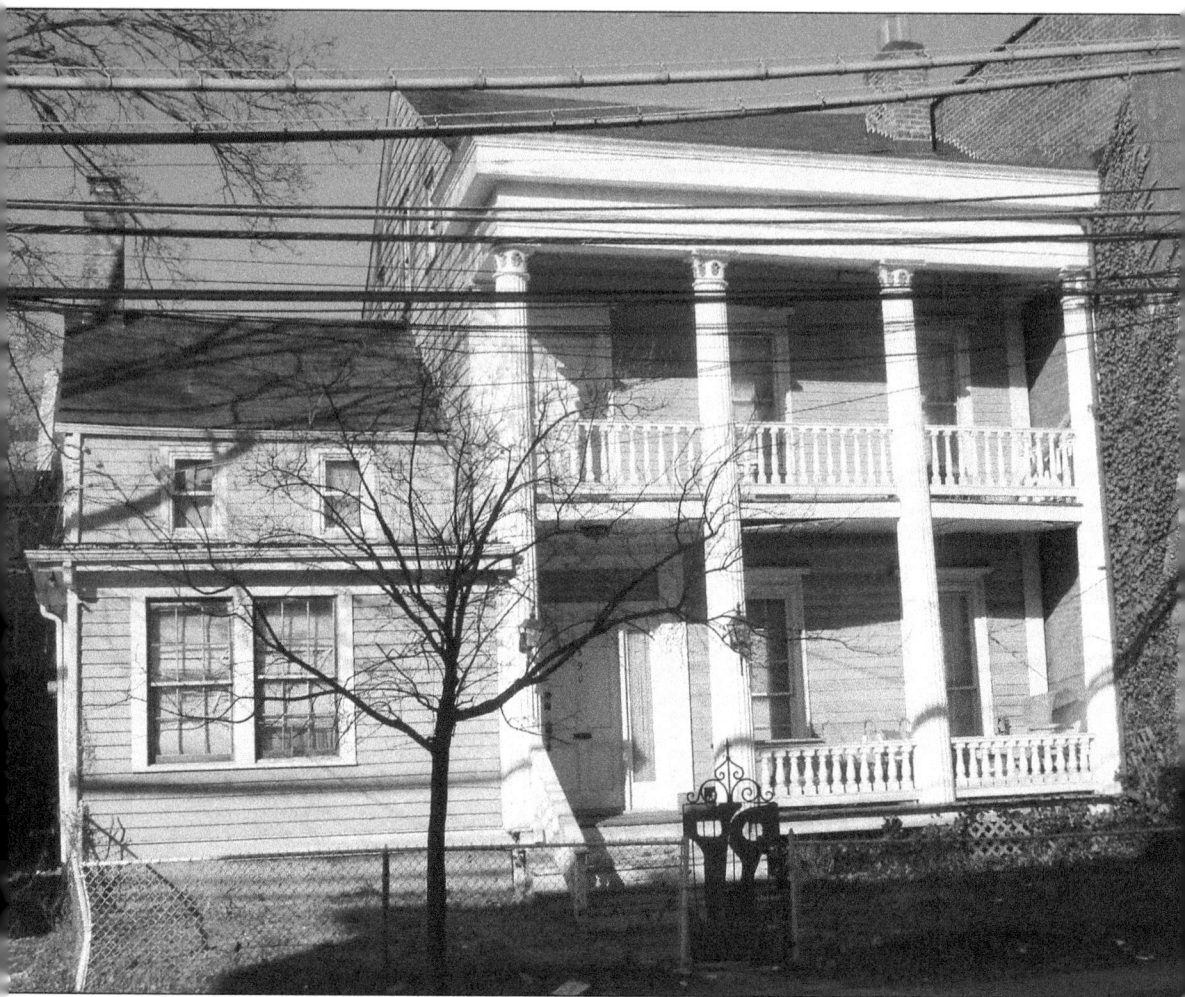

This 1835 frame Greek Revival–style house on Van Duzer Street still stands today and is a New York City Landmark. It was built by Richard Smith, whose wife was a daughter of Vice Pres. Daniel D. Tompkins. (David Goldfarb collection.)

This splendid Greek Revival home was the first to be erected on Harrison Street. In 1835, Susan and Richard Smith purchased some building lots, and by around 1840, they had built their classically inspired home. Susan Smith was the daughter of governor and former vice president Daniel D. Tompkins and was the sister of the Village of Stapleton cofounder, Minthorn Tompkins. Considered to be one of the most important homes in all of Stapleton, it has been lovingly restored by the current owners who purchased the historic property in 1977. (David Goldfarb collection.)

One of the oldest extant buildings in Stapleton is at 172 St. Paul's Avenue. It was built around 1830 as the rectory for the first church building for St. Paul's Episcopal Church, which was demolished in 1870. (David Goldfarb collection.)

General store owners Edward and Amelia Blake built this imposing home on Harrison Street around 1845. It was subsequently owned by noted Stapleton attorney Theodore Frean, who purchased the home about 1869. (David Goldfarb collection.)

This impressive Italianate home belonged to Dr. W. C. Anderson, one of the men associated with the burning of the quarantine station. Dr. Anderson started the *Sepoy*, a newspaper, in 1859 at Stapleton. The intent of the paper was to defend the people of Staten Island from unjust attacks in the aftermath of the burning of the quarantine. It was published every Saturday until the issue of the moving of the quarantine was resolved. Dr. Anderson suggested the use of a "floating" hospital ship similar to one that was being used off London at the time. In the paper, Dr. Anderson is referred to as being "experienced in management of hospital, especially of the treatment of Yellow Fever Patients." George M. Root was later the editor, and he went on to start the *Gazette* when the *Sepoy* folded in June 1859. (Staten Island Museum Collection.)

The landmark Boardman-Mitchell House faces Bay Street, but its lot continues through to Brownell Street. The home is a rare surviving example of an early Italianate villa. Built in 1848, it is situated on a steep bluff above Bay Street. The Boardman and Mitchell families owned the house for 120 years. The photograph below shows two arch-top casement windows on the third floor of the home looking out onto the harbor with an extensive view of the Manhattan skyline. The house has several window styles, including tall French windows, faux casement windows, small casement windows, and hopper windows. (David Goldfarb collection.)

This image shows the imposing entrance hall of the Boardman-Mitchell House, which overlooks Bay Street. The original owner, Dr. James R. Boardman, served as resident physician at the nearby Seaman's Retreat Hospital from 1836 to 1844 and again in 1849. Boardman was an early investor in Staten Island real estate. The home's second owner, Capt. Elvin Eugene Mitchell, was a Sandy Hook pilot. Lelia Lee Roberts owned this stately home from 1978 until her death in 2009, at which time it was bequeathed to historian Barnett Shepard, who is currently restoring it. (David Goldfarb collection.)

This beautiful Greek Revival–style home at 63 William Street was completed around 1844. The house was built by fisherman David Burgher, who also served on the town council and as a deputy sheriff in the mid-19th century, a time when the ferries and ports in Stapleton made for an attractive location for early suburban development. (David Goldfarb collection.)

Four

VICTORIAN STAPLETON

As the 19th century progressed, every style of architecture that came in and went out of fashion was represented in the prosperous village of Stapleton—from the bracketed Italianate villa and the Gothic Revival cottage to the idiosyncratic Queen Anne, continuing to the Colonial Revival as well as the shingle-style home.

One of the grandest homes built late in the 19th century that still stands is the unqualified queen of St. Paul's Avenue—No. 387, built by beer baron George Bechtel as a wedding gift for his daughter. This confection of a structure features a "consumption porch," three-story tower, shingles of many configurations, Queen Anne–type windows, and stained glass at the double front doors; in fact, the house contained all the latest accoutrement available to the home builder at the end of the 19th century.

Diagonally across St. Paul's Avenue from the Bechtel home stands another spectacular home. Built early in the 20th century, the massive Zentgraf Mansion, at the corner of Occident and St. Paul's Avenues, is one of the largest residential structures still extant within the boundaries of Stapleton. This sprawling arts and crafts–style home was built by the president of the successful paper manufacturing firm, Louis DeJonge and Company.

A walk around the sloping terrain within the St. Paul's Avenue-Stapleton Heights Historic district, as well as the streets bordering, is truly an American architectural history lesson in three dimensions.

This image shows the magnificent Hormann Castle, with its terraced lawns sloping steeply toward the bay. August Hormann built his Rhineland Castle in Stapleton Heights to capture the incredible views of the Narrows as well as those of Stapleton, where his Rubsam and Hormann Brewery was located. The "castle" lasted well into the 20th century but was demolished in the 1970s to make way for the housing development known as Howard Circle. (Staten Island Museum Collection.)

One can discern the quality of Stapleton as a 19th-century neighborhood from this photograph taken along St. Paul's Avenue. (Staten Island Museum Collection.)

The Queen Anne Bechtel-Wagner House was built by brewery baron George Bechtel as a wedding gift for his daughter, Anna, whose husband, Leonard Weiderer, owned a glass factory in Stapleton. Architect Hugo Kafka Sr. designed the home, which was built by Stapleton builder Henry Spruck. It is home today to Dr. Ted and Donna Brown and their children. Dr. Brown was the president of the Mud Lane Society for the Renaissance of Stapleton. (Dr. W. Ted Brown collection.)

The Louis A. and Laura Stirn House is a New York City Landmark. It is a neo-Renaissance–style mansion with arts and crafts–styled details designed by Kafka and Lindermeyr and built in 1908 by Henry Spruck and Son. The home, one of the few houses of this style and size surviving on Staten Island, is prominently located on Howard Avenue on Grymes Hill. (James G. Ferreri collection.)

Built around 1891 from a design attributed to Paul Kuhne, an architect with offices in Stapleton and Manhattan, this Renaissance Revival–style home suffered a fire in the 1940s and was rebuilt as seen today. This home, at 368 St. Paul's Avenue, was originally built for importer Adolph Baddenhausen and his wife, Minnie. (David Goldfarb collection.)

This massive mid-19th-century Italianate home was built elsewhere and moved to its current location at 417 St. Paul's Avenue around 1886 by John Steiner, a Stapleton merchant. Steiner, who built six homes along St. Paul's Avenue, left this house to his daughter. Margaretha Steiner married Edward Meurer, a descendant of one of the oldest Huguenot families on Staten Island, and the home remained in the Meurer family until 1957. (James G. Ferreri collection.)

Built between 1908 and 1909, this colossal dwelling at 400 St. Paul's Avenue was designed by Otto Loeffler, a native of Staten Island who was responsible for building nearly one dozen homes in the Stapleton historic district. The arts and crafts home was built for Ernest W. Zentgraf who was a principal in the Dejonge Paper Company, an important manufacturing concern on Staten Island at the time. (David Goldfarb collection.)

Built around 1883, which was quite late in the period for a Second Empire–style home, this graceful structure commands one of the best views in Stapleton from its vantage point at the corner of St. Paul's Avenue and Beach Street. Note the wooden wraparound porch with bracketed and fluted columns and the three-story square tower at a 45 degree angle from the main facade. (David Goldfarb collection.)

This Second Empire–style house at 351 St. Paul's Avenue was built around 1887 for William Hechler, chief chemist and brewmaster at the Bechtel Brewery. It later became the home of prominent Staten Islanders Pearse and Catherine (Mac) O'Callaghan. Note the slate mansard roof and the three-story tower. (Courtesy of Catherine O'Callaghan.)

Pearse O'Callaghan was chair of the liberal party of Richmond County and commissioner of cemeteries under Gov. Mario Cuomo. Here Pearse is shown in February 1995 following a bagpiper into his dining room. Among the many candidates who ran on the liberal line was New York City mayor Rudy Guliani, shown below at an event at the O'Callaghan home. "Mac" O'Callaghan and the Rev. Terry Troia of Project Hospitality are on the right. (Courtesy of Catherine O'Callaghan.)

This wonderful, decorative brick Victorian at 53 Harrison Street was built around 1880 by Henry Warth, the scion of a banking family. (David Goldfarb collection.)

This diminutive Second Empire–styled home at 59 Harrison Street was built around 1870 by carpenter/builder brothers Adrian and Peter Post, who were responsible for a few homes on this block. (David Goldfarb collection.)

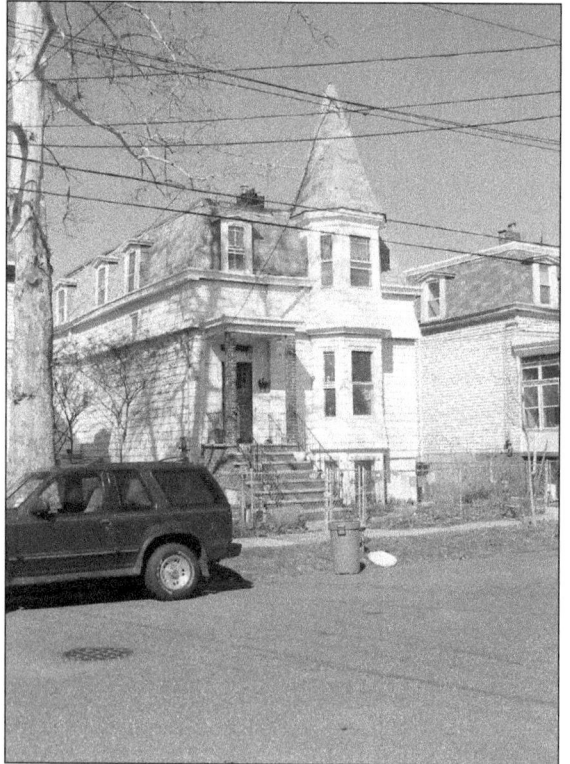

A central towered bay ending in a witches cap roof is the distinguishing characteristic in the Second Empire home dating from around 1869 and built by the Post brothers. (David Goldfarb collection.)

Another small home of the mansard roof variety on Harrison Street boasts a central bay on the facade with two roof dormers. The home was built in 1868 by Michael J. Tynan, a dealer in coal and wood. (David Goldfarb collection.)

The homes at 75 (to the right) and 77 Harrison Street show how in demand lots had become by the late 1880s, due to the close proximity of the two houses. The *c.* 1868 petite mansard roof home that was built by the Post brothers sports a single roof dormer, while the *c.* 1883 2.5-story home, built by Sarah L. Wood, a news dealer, has been shoehorned in next door. (David Goldfarb collection.)

Attached row houses are a rarity on Staten Island, as opposed to the other four boroughs of Greater New York, where the freestanding wood-frame home would be the peculiarity. Here these two *c.* 1877 buildings stand on land that was originally owned by the Smiths from their 1835 purchase of building lots. Nos. 83 and 85 Harrison Street were built by Isabella and Samuel Cassidy, who were dry goods merchants. The couple lived at No. 83 and rented No. 85 to tenants. (David Goldfarb collection.)

This stunning *c.* 1883 double house was erected by builder Phillip Wolf as an investment property at 87–89 Harrison Street. This house, along with its neighbor at 93–95 Harrison Street, also built by Wolf, were considered premier rental addresses in their day. (David Goldfarb collection.)

This terrific view of the double house at 93–95 Harrison Street shows the care and quality that was invested into speculative properties during the last quarter of the 19th century. (David Goldfarb collection.)

This home at 34 Quinn Street represents hundreds of surviving examples on Staten Island in its diminutive size so typical of the 1850s. (David Goldfarb collection.)

The home at the center of the image, 54 Quinn Street, was built in 1894 by developer Charles L. Wolff. (David Goldfarb collection.)

Another home built by Wolff at 52 Quinn Street, also constructed of brick, shows his concern for a street's character, by varying the styles of adjoining homes. (David Goldfarb collection.)

The homes at 25 to 31 Tompkins Street show the development of this part of Stapleton. Those to the right of the image date from the early 1880s, while the home at the center is either very late 19th or early 20th century. The fourth home from the right was built in the middle of the 19th century. (David Goldfarb collection.)

Although it is boarded up and crumbling, this home at 15 Tompkins Street shows the hallmarks of Colonial Revival architecture in America. Note the Palladian window on the large front gable, the oval in the smaller gable, the pediment above the steps, as well as the one surviving classical column. (David Goldfarb collection.)

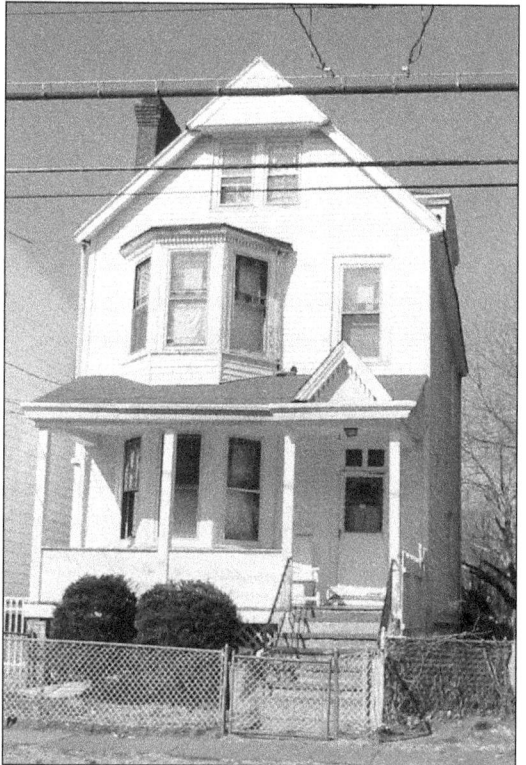

A layer of vinyl cannot hide the classical elements built onto this home at 17 Tompkins Street. It is a transitional home built as a Queen Anne but also showing classical elements. Note the multipaned Queen Anne windows in the second floor bay and the dentils above. (David Goldfarb collection.)

This lovely home at 61 Tompkins Street would be considered a "Free Classic Queen Anne." Note the paired classical columns, the pediment above the steps with dentil detailing, and a classical wreath and garland motif at its center. (David Goldfarb collection.)

Although altered, many Victorian-era details are still visible on the home at 65 Tompkins Street. Note the roof brackets. (David Goldfarb collection.)

There are two stylish double brick houses on Harrison Street. The double house at the right of the image is 81 Harrison Street, built around 1876 by Mary Ann and Samuel Anderson, a notary and landlord. While St. Paul's Avenue and Stapleton Heights seemed to have been the domain of the brewery owners, the brewmasters, and the wealthier business families, the Harrison and Quinn Street vicinity, sometimes known as "the nook," became the home of a growing middle class of factory workers, many of them tenants in stylish wooden and brick Victorian homes. (David Goldfarb collection.)

Five

BREWERIES

If ever there was a perfect community in which to brew beer, it was Stapleton.

Blessed with clear and cold artesian springs, as well as ancient caves that rimmed the westerly hills of the village, caves that had hidden Hessian soldiers during the Revolutionary War, Stapleton was deemed ideal by the many German immigrants who brought their beer-making talents to the village.

Local lore has it that Italian liberator Giuseppi Garibaldi and his friend, inventor of the telephone, Antonio Meucci, founded the first brewery on Staten Island in 1851. This may be apocryphal, but the two did lend their names, if not their knowledge, to one of the earliest beer-making ventures on the island.

With the German political upheavals of the 1840s, hundreds of German immigrants settled on Staten Island, mostly in Stapleton and nearby Clifton. The first brewery to settle in the area was known as the Clifton Brewery, located near the Vanderbilt ferry landing. After changing hands a few times, this brewery was bought by Bachmann, whose brew became popular in the New York and New Jersey areas. In 1853, John Bechtel founded his brewery at the top of Broad Street and Richmond Road, today's Van Duzer Street. Bechtel soon expanded the brewery building and constructed a state-of-the-art stable for his delivery horses in the basement. Bechtel's son, George, oversaw the family brewing business with such acumen, that he became Staten Island's largest taxpayer. Bechtel's beer was so good that when the Japanese ambassador visited Staten Island in 1879, he ordered 100,000 bottles to be sent to Japan. No surprise since Bechtel's beer had already won gold medals across the United States and Europe.

Later in the 1850s came another beer plant, eventually known as Bischoff's. Joseph Rubsam and August Hormann began brewing beer around 1870 in Stapleton. This partnership would produce a lager that would win top honors at the American Centennial Exhibition in Philadelphia in 1876.

The Stapleton breweries suffered during Prohibition, and most did not survive. Rubsam and Hormann was bought by the Piel's Company and lasted into the mid-20th century, while Bechtel's factory was destroyed in a blazing inferno in 1931.

The colossal scale of George Bechtel's brewery is evident from this photograph and early sketch. Bechtel built a state-of-the-art stable across Van Duzer Street from the brewery proper, to house his many horses that were used for delivering Bechtel's lager across the city. The basement of the stables included tubs for washing the horses indoors. The stable building still stands, one last reminder of the days when Stapleton was the center of beer brewing in the area. Today the stable building houses a religious organization. (Above, David Goldfarb collection; below, Staten Island Museum Collection.)

This image is the lager beer trademark of Bechtel Brewery. In 1885, George Bechtel registered a trademark for lager beer with the U.S. Patent Office. Lager beer is fermented at a much lower temperature and with different yeast than other beers. Cold storage of beer or "lagering" is often done in cool cellars or caves. (Dr. W. Ted Brown collection.)

Employees of the George Bechtel Brewery are surrounding barrels of his famous lager beer in this image. George Bechtel was hugely successful in his Stapleton operation and was, for many years, Staten Island's largest taxpayer. While the brewery owner lived in Stapleton Heights, many of his employees lived in more modest houses in lower Stapleton, in areas such as Harrison and Quinn Streets. (David Goldfarb collection.)

BACHMANN'S CLIFTON BREWERY
— CIRCA 1900

BIRDS EYE VIEW OF
THE BACHMANN BREWING Cº CLIFTON, S.I.

The first brewing venture on Staten Island was the Clifton Brewery. Legend attributes its original ownership to Italian inventor Antonio Meucci and Italian liberator Giuseppe Garibaldi. After passing through several owners, it was acquired by Bachmann and became very popular throughout the region. It later became Bachmann-Bechtel Brewery of Clifton and is depicted here in 1911 on the annual report of the Staten Island Chamber of Commerce. (Dr. W. Ted Brown collection.)

As other prominent Staten Island families had done, the Bechtel's built an imposing mausoleum. The Bechtel Mausoleum is located in nearby Silver Mount Cemetery. (James G. Ferreri collection.)

78

The R and H Brewery (formerly Rubsam and Hormann) is decorated for an event, with bunting at the windows and pennant flags cascading from the roofline to the ground. The plant was later bought by Piels and operated until 1963. (Staten Island Museum Collection.)

August Hormann founded the Atlantic Brewery in 1870 along with his partner, Joseph Rubsam. The name of the company was soon changed to Rubsam and Hormann and eventually to R and H. In December 1953, the Piels Brothers Company bought the plant of Rubsam and Hormann in Stapleton, as well as the R and H label. However, by 1963, as sales of the Piels brand slowed, the R and H plant was closed. (Staten Island Museum Collection.)

An R and H Brewery cart is parked in front of the massive plant. Note the signs near and on the cart advertising the Old Style Hotel, which was located near the plant grounds. In the late 19th century, people often made the journey from other parts of the metropolitan area to the many superior breweries on Staten Island to spend the day picnicking and partaking of the cool, clear lagers available here. (Staten Island Museum Collection.)

Piels Brewery is visible in this *c.* 1962 shot of Canal Street. Piels was still a huge presence among the smaller commercial structures. Note the sign along the cornice of the tower that announces "Piels Beer." Notice also Trunz Meats, the chain that had outlets in almost every shopping area of Staten Island among its 85 stores, then located in Brooklyn, Queens, and Long Island as well. The Trunz Pork Stores were founded in Greenpoint, Brooklyn, in 1904 by German immigrant Max Trunz and later became known as Trunz Meats. (Staten Island Museum Collection.)

The fire at the Bachmann-Bechtel Brewery on Van Duzer Street at the top of Broad Street, which began at 1:10 a.m. on Tuesday, February 3, 1931, is pictured in this image. The inferno soon spread to several adjoining buildings. Twenty-five fire companies from other boroughs joined island firefighters in attempting to control the blaze. The brewery had been inactive for 12 years at the time of the fire. This is a World Wide Photo of the fire. (Dr. W. Ted Brown collection.)

A very early cartoon sketch shows beer barrels being stored in the cool caves in the Stapleton hillside. Lager beer is fermented at a much lower temperature and with different yeast than other beer. Cold storage of beer or "lagering" is often done in cool cellars or caves. (Staten Island Museum Collection.)

Demyan's Hofbrau House opened at the site of the Bechtel Brewery in 1959, after the original location that the Demyan family opened in 1955 in Stapleton burned. The eatery was a huge draw from all parts of the island for decades until it was lost in a dramatic blaze in 1980. (Dr. W. Ted Brown collection.)

Were these gentlemen enjoying a Staten Island brew? Perhaps, but most significant is the fact that the portrait hanging above the bar behind the threesome is of Admiral Dewey, the hero of the Spanish-American War. Adm. George Dewey was best known for his victory without the loss of a single life of his own forces due to combat; only one man died, of heat stroke, at the Battle of Manila Bay. Since the Spanish-American War took place between April and August 1898, this photograph can be placed sometime later. (Staten Island Museum Collection.)

Six

Buildings for Public Use

In 1866, Stapleton, Clifton, and a portion of Tompkinsville were incorporated into the Village of Edgewater. In 1889, the Edgewater Village Hall was erected at the rear of Washington Square, today's Tappen Park.

The U.S. Marine Hospital was built along the Stapleton shore. The National Institutes of Health began as a single-room laboratory of hygiene for bacteriological investigation, established by the U.S. Marine Hospital Service in Stapleton, Staten Island, New York, in 1887.

In the years prior to the Civil War, Stapleton's ports were busy in trade with the Southern states. In the midst of the war, abolitionist Francis Gould Shaw, financier Louis H. Meyer, and brewer John Bechtel, along with 18 other area businessmen, incorporated the Staten Island Savings Bank.

The first bank building, operating in rented commercial space, was located on Bay Street at Broad Street; it soon relocated to the Tynan Building at the corner of Dock and Bay Streets. The bank then moved to a Second Empire–styled building at Beach and Water Streets that had served as the original Edgewater Village Hall. The building was demolished in 1922 to make way for a new, stunning neoclassical building that occupies the site today.

Church structures also played an important role in the Stapleton community, and within its boundaries today stand two exquisite examples of church architecture—St. Paul's Memorial Episcopal Church and Trinity Lutheran Church. Trinity Lutheran Church was founded in 1856 to serve the influx of German immigrants to Stapleton. The new church built on the site was begun in 1913 in the Gothic style.

Along with banks and churches, Stapleton also is home to a branch of the New York City Public Library, built in 1907 as one of the Carnegie-donated library branches.

Before there were fire alarm boxes, bell towers were erected to alert the populace in the event a fire occurred. This bell tower was located between Water and Canal Streets. Below is another view of the Stapleton fire bell, this time in a winter scene complete with bare trees and ice in the foreground. A horse and buggy and trolley travel in opposite directions, as an elderly gentleman braves the frozen road. (Staten Island Museum Collection.)

Village Hall, Stapleton, Staten Island, N.Y.

In 1866, Stapleton, Clifton, and a portion of Tompkinsville were incorporated into the Village of Edgewater. In the years before the consolidation of Greater New York in 1898, these incorporated villages covered all five boroughs. In 1889, the Edgewater Village Hall, designed by Paul Kuhne, was erected at the rear of Washington Square, today's Tappen Park. The Edgewater Village Hall is one of only two village halls still standing in New York City. The picture above is the village hall around 1907. Note the many arch-topped windows and bracketed eaves that give the building its unique beauty. Below, the village hall is at the extreme left of this photograph of the town square. (David Goldfarb collection.)

The hand-written note on the postcard reads:

Having a fine time down here. The air is fine. Thank you for your postal. Grandma sends her love as do all the rest. Ethel

The beautiful campus of the U.S. Marine Hospital was built along the Stapleton shore. The National Institutes of Health began as a single-room laboratory of hygiene for bacteriological investigation, established by the U.S Marine Hospital Service at Stapleton, Staten Island, New York, in 1887. From 1887 to 1891, the laboratory was located in the attic of the Marine Hospital on Staten Island, which had been the charity Seaman's Retreat until it was leased by the federal government in 1883 and made part of the Marine Hospital Service. The image below shows the old stone house on the grounds of the Marine Hospital. (Above, Staten Island Museum Collection; below, David Goldfarb collection.)

These are two lovely views of the U.S. Marine Hospital and surrounding grounds. The image below is from the 19th century while the above photograph is from the first quarter of the 20th century. (David Goldfarb collection.)

Main Building   New U. S. Marine Hospital   Stapleton, S. I., N. Y.

The "new" main building at the U.S. Marine Hospital is pictured here around 1937. (David Goldfarb collection.)

AERIAL VIEW, U. S. MARINE HOSPITAL, STAPLETON, STATEN ISLAND, N. Y.

This aerial view of the U.S. Marine Hospital dates from around 1949. (David Goldfarb collection.)

By 1884, all competing ferry services to Staten Island had been sold to the Baltimore and Ohio Railroad and operated by the Staten Island Rapid Transit Railroad, a plan implemented by Erastus Wiman along with his partners, William Pendleton and Robert Garrett. Garrett was president of the railroad. Wiman's plan included connecting the ferries with the rail lines and moving the ferry terminal to St. George. Above is the Staten Island Rapid Transit at the Stapleton Train Station and below is the Vanderbilt Avenue Train Station. (Above, David Goldfarb collection; below Staten Island Museum Collection.)

Designed by prolific Staten Island architect Edward Alfred Sargent around 1901, this monumental building was constructed to house the Tompkins Lodge No. 471, a Masonic Hall, on the second floor while it housed a post office on the street level beginning in 1903. The original design had two corner towers and an open balcony at the center of the second-floor facade. The interior boasted a stunning central meeting room with coffered ceiling and massive dome. The building still stands, though greatly altered. (Staten Island Museum Collection.)

These are two postcard views of the New York Public Library Branch. The Stapleton Branch of the New York Public Library opened in 1907 and is located on Canal Street, near the center of Stapleton Village, skirting Tappen Park and the Old Village Hall. It was one of the many library buildings in the city constructed with funds provided by Andrew Carnegie. The graceful building was designed by Carrere and Hastings. Above is from the Valentine and Sons Publishing Company Ltd., and below is from the Greenville Merchandise Company of Jersey City. (Both, David Goldfarb collection.)

The Stapleton Courthouse at Rocky Hollow (as this area of Staten Island was once known), at 67 Targee Street, serves as the criminal court building for Staten Island today. It was built after the consolidation of Greater New York. Each of the five boroughs that comprise Greater New York has or had one criminal court building constructed contemporaneously with the Staten Island branch. This postcard view is from around 1933. (Dr. W. Ted Brown collection.)

Public School No. 14, shown around 1907, was designed by Edward Alfred Sargent at Broad and Brook Streets. Sargent designed many of the public school buildings on Staten Island during this period, including P. S. 15, which is a New York City Designated Landmark on St. Paul's Avenue. (David Goldfarb collection.)

Public School No. 14, Stapleton, S. I.

Another view of Sargent's P. S. 14 shows the details that were so typical of public school design during this period. Edward Alfred Sargent was one of the most prolific architects working on Staten Island at the time, and his work can be seen in both of the island's designated residential historic districts, Stapleton and St. George. (David Goldfarb collection.)

Stapleton schoolchildren seated around their teacher are pictured early in the 20th century. (Staten Island Museum Collection.)

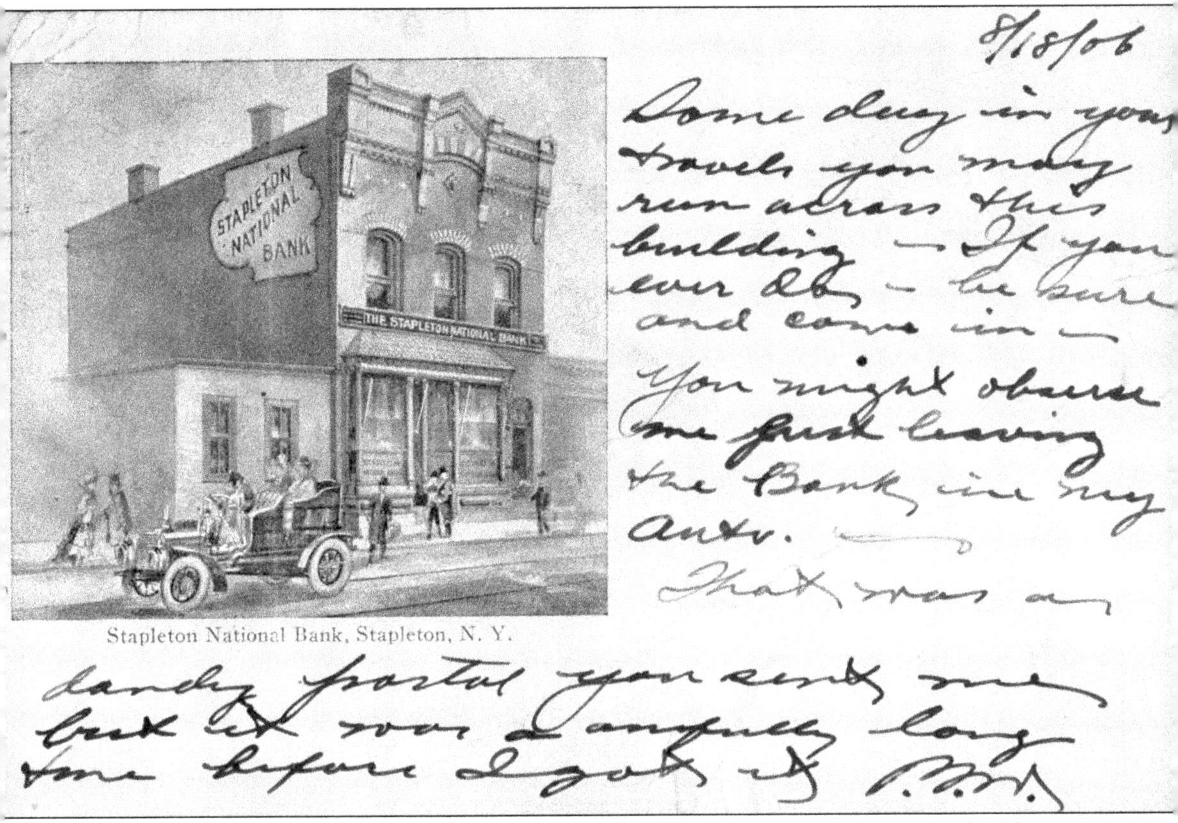

Established in 1904, the National Bank of Stapleton was located on Bay Street in a building that still stands today. The postcard is dated August 18, 1906, and the sender has written: "Some day in your travels, you may run across this building—If you ever do—be sure to come in—you might just observe me leaving the bank in my auto. That was a dandy postal you sent me but it was an awfully long time before I got it." Seems postal service was slow then, too? (Staten Island Museum Collection.)

These are two views of the Second Empire–styled building that was an early home to the Staten Island Savings Bank. In the midst of the Civil War, abolitionist Francis Gould Shaw, financier Louis H. Meyer, and brewer John Bechtel, along with 18 other area businessmen, incorporated the Staten Island Savings Bank. The first bank building was rented commercial space located on Bay Street at Broad Street but soon relocated to the Tynan Building at the corner of Dock and Bay Streets. The bank then moved to a triangular lot at the corner at Beach and Water Streets. The Second Empire–styled building pictured here had served as the original Edgewater Village Hall. The bank occupied the structure until it was demolished in 1922 to make way for a new bank building. (Above, Staten Island Museum Collection; below, David Goldfarb collection.)

Here are two views of the present-day Staten Island Savings Bank. In the early 1920s, it was announced that a new structure, to be designed by Delano and Aldridge, would be built in the heart of Stapleton. (Above, Staten Island Museum Collection; below, David Goldfarb collection.)

The wonderful carvings that adorned the Liberty Theater's facade include cornucopia with cascading fruit. The Liberty Theater on Beach Street was designed by Staten Island architect James Whitford and was opened in 1918 by veteran showman Charles Moses. The year 1919 was a huge year for this theater, with a solid parade of such performers as Fred Allen, Victor Moore, George Raft, Sophie Tucker, Georgie Jessel, and Ben Bernie. By the late 1920s, motion pictures succeeded the stage shows at the theater. (Staten Island Museum Collection.)

The massive wood-frame Richmond Theater, as it appeared around 1908, was one of the many theaters located throughout Stapleton. (Dr. W. Ted Brown collection.)

Opened in October 1930 and built basically in front of the Vanderbilt mansion, the Paramount Theater was considered the second most prestigious theater on Staten Island (second only to the spectacular St. George Theater). Its original design was unique; it had a Wurlitzer theater organ with two consoles, one of only 10 such installations in the United States. A four-week, $135,000 renovation in 1961 resulted in its reopening as the New Paramount Theater, with wider seats and aisles and a seating capacity of 2,000. By September 1980, the movie theater closed its doors, and the building was used as a nightclub, named, what else, the Paramount. The nightclub had a short life, and the theater reopened as a rock concert venue, lasting just a few years. There are currently plans underway by the current owner to restore the facade of the beautiful art deco structure. (Staten Island Museum Collection.)

Although the location is not certain, this 1915 image of the Elk's Club in Stapleton clearly shows the elegant communities that made up a good portion of the area. Notice the large bronze elk statue on the front lawn. (Staten Island Museum Collection.)

The Old Ladies' Home, Stapleton.   Richmond Borough, N. Y.

The "Old Ladies Home" was actually the Mariners' Family Asylum at 119 Tompkins Avenue, the only facility in New York City dedicated to the care of the wives, mothers, sisters, and daughters of seamen. Organized by the Mariners' Family Industrial Society, the home was constructed in 1852–1853 and opened in 1854. The stunning Italianate gem was demolished in 2009 to make way for a new home for the New York Founding Hospital. (Dr. W. Ted Brown collection.)

The original St. Paul's Episcopal Church, a wood-frame structure, was built on land donated by Caleb T. Ward in the 1840s. In 1865, his son, Albert, commissioned a new stone church for the parishioners, provided they be responsible for erecting a suitable rectory. He saw the new church as "a fitting monument to the honor and sacred memory of his departed sister." The commission for both buildings went to Edward Tuckerman Potter, who designed them in the High Victorian Gothic style. St. Paul's is considered one of the most beautiful church campuses in the country. The church and rectory are triple-landmarked, meaning they are protected by a New York City Landmarks designation, as well as being on the state and federal registers of historic places. (Above, Staten Island Museum Collection; below, collection of Dr. W. Ted Brown.)

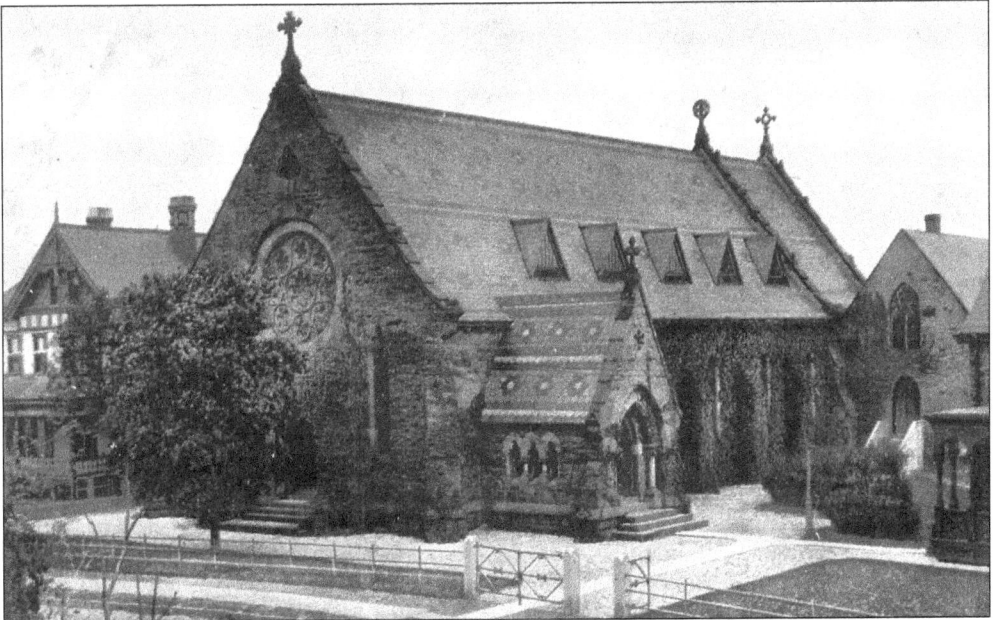

1856. Zur Erinnerung 1906.

....an das....

50-JAEHRIGE JUBILAEUM

...der...

Deutschen Evangelisch-Lutherischen Gemeinde

...zu...

STAPLETON, - - STATEN ISLAND,

NEW YORK.

Trinity Lutheran Church was founded in 1856 to serve the influx of German immigrants to Stapleton. At the close of the Civil War, the German Lutheran Congregation that had been holding meetings at the nearby Kingsley Methodist Church purchased two lots at the corner of Beach Street and St. Paul's Avenue. Albert Ward donated two additional lots in order to allow enough land for the wood-frame building that the congregation purchased from the Unitarian church and moved to the site from the corner of Cebra Avenue and Victory Boulevard. This small church with central spire served the community until 1913. (Staten Island Museum Collection.)

The new and much larger church built on the site was begun in 1913 in the Gothic style and features gargoyles at the four corners of the tower. A stunning view taken looking up at Trinity Lutheran Church shows the masterful Gothic-style elements such as crenellated parapets and Gothic arches, not to mention the fanciful avian gargoyles at the corners that were built onto the 20th-century church. (Staten Island Museum Collection.)

This chancel view inside Trinity Lutheran Church shows the Rev. Frederic Sutter and the Rev. Carl Sutter. (Dr. W. Ted Brown collection.)

This view of an entrance to Trinity Lutheran Church shows the Gothic-style elements such as parapets and Gothic arches. (Dr. W. Ted Brown collection.)

Trinity Church is shown with its Richard Meyer Memorial Organ and Luther stained-glass window, made for the church in Munich, Germany. (Dr. W. Ted Brown collection.)

Formerly the First Presbyterian Church at Brownell and Tompkins Streets, this building today is occupied by the Mount Sinai United Christian Church. (David Goldfarb collection.)

This building, located on Brownell Street, is currently vacant. Standing opposite the United Christian Church across Tompkins Street, the once lovely building has been greatly altered; a coating of stucco has been applied to the exterior, and most windows are currently covered with boards. (David Goldfarb collection.)

Built around 1887, Immaculate Conception Roman Catholic Church at 128 Targee Street displays the exuberance common to most late-19th-century church structures; from the massive Corinthian columns to the square corner campanile, the stunning church structure is a grand presence in 21st century Stapleton. (David Goldfarb collection.)

Looking to establish a new Baptist church on Staten Island, the Rev. Purcell Brown and Deacon Hilton Holcombe acquired a vacant Jewish synagogue at 119 Wright Street in Stapleton. In October 1978, the first small group entered the building on Wright Street for worship, constituting the beginning of First Central Baptist church. (David Goldfarb collection.)

Seven

THE STAPLETON "STAPES"

The Staten Island "Stapletons" was a football team founded in 1915 by local businessman Dan Blaine, as a neighborhood team, with Blaine serving as the halfback. In those days before World War I, the Stapletons played other neighborhood semipro teams in the New York City area, winning several semipro titles. Each team player received a $10 bill per game as salary.

Due to Blaine's service in the military, the Stapletons were idle during 1918 but were renewed by 1919, at which time Blaine was owner of the team, retiring as a player in 1924 while continuing in his dual capacity as owner and manager. It was in 1924, in fact, that the Stapletons claimed the New York Metropolitan championship. By this time the team was playing on their own field, Thompson Stadium, which stood where the Stapleton Houses housing project stands today.

By 1928, Dan Blaine wanted the Stapletons to be an NFL franchise team. Blaine signed Doug Wykoff as a player-coach, as well as six graduates from the nationally ranked New York University team.

After scoring a 10-1-1 record in 1928, Blaine applied in 1929 for an NFL franchise. In order to secure the franchise, Giants owner Tim Marra's permission was needed, since Staten Island was in his exclusive territory. Marra had an extra franchise, and after much wrangling, these franchise rights were granted to the Stapletons. Ken Strong, who became a Stapleton's Hall of Famer and who had received All-American honors while at NYU, was immediately hired to play on the team by Blaine. In July 1931, the team's official name on league records was changed from the Stapleton Football Club, Inc., to Staten Island Stapes.

The Stapes never had a winning season. In 1932, the team finished in last place. To make matters worse, their star player, Ken Strong, signed with the Giants and helped them win the NFL Championship that season.

The Stapes played one more season in 1934 before closing operations one year later. In June 1935, Blaine's franchise was declared forfeited, and blame for the team's failure can be attributed to the combination of the Great Depression, a time when few football fans had enough money to pay to watch the games, and the fact that Thompson Stadium was much too small a venue to accommodate enough fans to make the team profitable during its entire existence.

In 1954, a testimonial was held for Stapleton's founder, Daniel Blaine (1891–1958). The journal that was printed for the occasion contained photographs of the early teams, as well as pages of testimonials and best wishes sent to the man that brought a Staten Island team into the National Football League for the first and only time. This image is of the cover of the journal. (Courtesy of Daniel Blaine.)

We dedicate this volume to a fine man, a wonderful friend and a good sportsman, who has spent a great portion of his life and talents to the fostering and promotion of athletics on Staten Island.

You rate applause and admiration for your accomplishments, Dan Blaine, for you personify the finest precepts of sportsmanship on the Island.

May this occasion bring back many happy memories and may we wish you many, many more years of health and happiness.

DAN BLAINE TESTIMONIAL COMMITTEE

This Page Sponsored By

BOROUGH PRES. E. G. BAKER and his CABINET

A page from the journal, sponsored by then Staten Island borough president, E. G. Baker, and his cabinet, clearly displays the high esteem that Dan Blaine was held in by those who knew of the man and his deeds. (Courtesy of Daniel Blaine.)

Proclaims Oct. 28 'Dan Blaine Day'

Seated (L-R): Mario (Mike Mazie) Bessi, Borough President Baker, Jim Rogers.
Standing: Patrick J. Kelly, Nate Meyers, Connie Sullivan, Councilman
          Al Maniscalco and Nick DeJoy.

Borough president Baker, center with pen, signs a proclamation stating that October 28 was "Dan Blaine Day" on Staten Island. (Courtesy of Daniel Blaine.)

STATEN ISLAND F.C.-1911

While the Stapletons were still known as the Staten Island Football Club, this team photograph was taken in 1911. (Courtesy of Daniel Blaine.)

114

Another of the regional semipro teams was the Edgewater Athletic Club, shown here around 1905. (Courtesy of Daniel Blaine.)

David Libby, Mgr., Fred Hagemann, J. Finley, T. Conroy, Ed Faire, W. Middleton, W. Carr, Mgr., Ed Harson, J. Van Dam, J. McKittrick, J. Cain, Geo. Corbett, J. Gilmartin, R. Bleeker, Joe Kehoe, Capt. W. Jones, Robert McDowell, E. Mueller, J. Smith, and "Dude" Mascot.

The St. Paul Athletic Association was photographed in 1904 along with the team's mascot, "Dude." (Courtesy of Daniel Blaine.)

JACK NEVIN   DAVE SKUDIN

STAPES CLUB DOCTOR

THE OLD MAESTRO

John Bunyon

Bing Miller

Shown is a page from the journal *This is Your Life, Dan Blaine*, printed to celebrate Dan Blaine Day in the 1950s. The photograph is captioned, "The Old Maestro." Note the photograph of the "Stapes" doctor, E. J. Amoury. (Courtesy of Daniel Blaine.)

A very early image of the football club from Stapleton, taken in 1903, shows that year's team. (Courtesy of Daniel Blaine.)

STAPLETONS-1915
Top Row (L-R): Gene Devlin, John Steiner, Dan Blaine, Lex Hannan, Bugs Wesslock, Joe Thompson.
Middle Row: Alec Doerr, Frank Joseph, Tom Walsh, Gregory Robillard, Harry Smith
Bottom Row: Augie Sandusky, Billy Gilmartin, Cal Finley, Joe Eib, Kiteltas, Mush Salig.

The Stapletons are shown as they appeared in 1915. Dan Blaine is seated in the first row, third from the left. The same photograph was used for the team in 1916. (Courtesy of Daniel Blaine.)

117

Apparently when the football season ended, Thompson Stadium hosted baseball games, as seen in this early-20th-century photograph of a summer of baseball. Thompson Stadium stood about where the Stapleton Houses, a NYC Housing Authority Project, stand today. Note the sign that reads "Tompkins, the Clothier," advertising Tompkins Department Store in West New Brighton. Spectators lounge on the outfield grass, as a debonair gentleman with a cane and straw hat stands behind second base. (Staten Island Museum Collection.)

The fullback for the 1925–1926 "Stapes," Bill O'Regan is shown in this 1927 photograph. The caption from a 1950s-era journal states that O'Regan was "now an Admiral in the U.S. Navy." (Courtesy of Daniel Blaine.)

Eight

MODERN STAPLETON

The second half of the 20th century was not a great time in the history of Stapleton. After World War II, the piers that had been built in the 1920s along the Stapleton shoreline laid idle and crumbling, while the buildings that had housed the breweries were demolished one by one. As happened across America, the move away from central Main Street shopping areas compounded the downturn. People left the large antique homes for more modern suburban-type houses further south on Staten Island.

A Robert Moses superblock public housing project was built on Broad Street on the site of the old Thompson Stadium, while the area already suffered from a serious downturn in business investment. Stores fronting along the town park were empty or occupied by social service entities.

Into this scenario ventured young people looking for an affordable North Shore community in which to live and work. They were more than happy to buy up the old mansions and commercial buildings and began to restore both their homes and their community. By the 1970s, Stapleton was well on the road back to restoration. In 1977, the Mud Lane Society for the Renaissance of Stapleton was founded to promote and improve the village of Stapleton. It began hosting house tours to introduce a new generation to the splendor of what had been a very important community, an important piece of the Staten Island story. In 2004, the New York City Landmarks Preservation Commission designated St. Paul's Avenue as the Stapleton Heights Historic District.

In the 1980s, Naval Station New York was planned for the Stapleton piers. It was originally intended that the battleship *Iowa* was to be berthed in this homeport. The navy insisted on maintaining a nuclear weapons option for the battleship *Iowa*, which met with great resistance by Stapleton residents. By 1995, with the end of the cold war, military bases around the country closed and the Stapleton Homeport ceased operations.

Today the Stapleton of the 21st century is happily a vibrant community with its eyes set firmly on the future, while remaining respectful of its glorious past.

Built on the site of the former Thompson Stadium in 1962, the Stapleton Houses consist of six eight-story buildings with 693 apartments, housing approximately 2,148 residents. The entire site is spread over nearly 18 acres of Stapleton along Broad Street. The six buildings that comprise the New York City Housing Authority's Stapleton Houses have exterior "halls" with apartment entrances from these catwalks. This one element gives this, Staten Island's largest housing project, some lovely views of the surrounding hills and waterfront. (David Goldfarb collection.)

A wonderful addition to the streetscape on Bay Street, this commercial structure fits in beautifully with the surrounding historic buildings. This aerial view shows the Staten Island Rapid Transit tracks behind the buildings with the Narrows in the distance. (David Goldfarb collection.)

New construction lines Broad Street near the site of the housing project, showing that the growth of Stapleton continues into the new millennium. (David Goldfarb collection.)

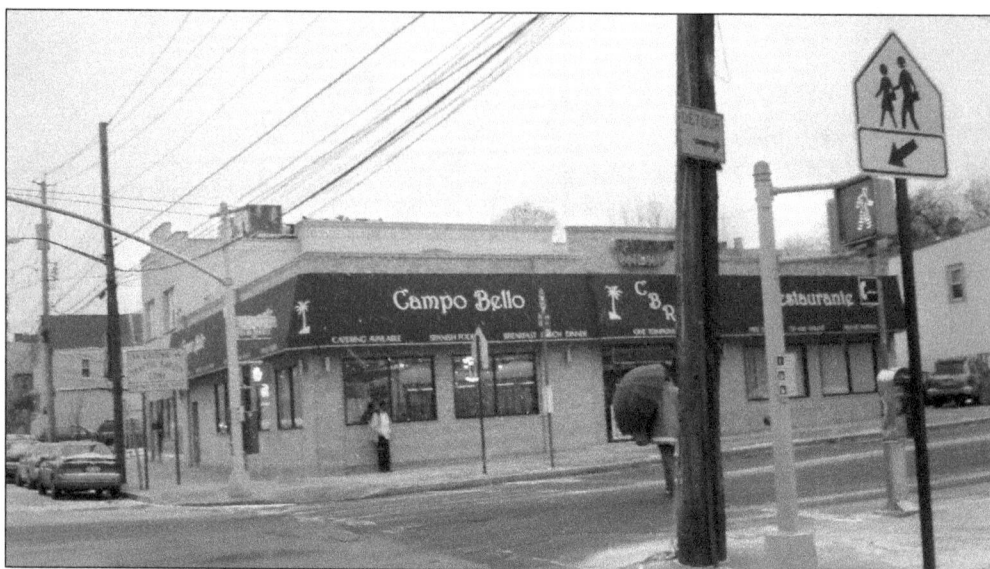

At the corner of Broad Street and Tompkins Avenue stands a newer building that is home to a successful Hispanic restaurant, a sure sign that Stapleton is a community that is still vital and growing. (David Goldfarb collection.)

A one-story taxpayer building housing a Subway restaurant at the corner of Bay and Wright Streets coexists alongside the taller buildings constructed in the 19th century during the years when Stapleton was an important shopping destination. (David Goldfarb collection.)

A branch of Chase Manhattan Bank was built during the mid-20th century on Bay Street between Canal and Wright Streets to serve the bustling Stapleton community. The building faces Tappen Park, with its back to the Narrows. (David Goldfarb collection.)

Brand-new construction at the rear of Tappen Park is shown as pictured in 2009. This three-story building was commenced before the recession that began in late 2008 and stands empty awaiting an upturn in the economy that will lead to it becoming an important asset to the main shopping area around the square. (David Goldfarb collection.)

Modern townhouses built along Wright Street stand as evidence that the Stapleton of today still is considered a desirable and affordable community. (David Goldfarb collection.)

This large McDonald's restaurant stands on Bay Street at Wave Street. Stapleton has its share of small, family-owned eateries and national chains throughout the community. (David Goldfarb collection.)

These are two views of the buildings that once housed the navy homeport along Front Street. There have been many failed attempts to adapt the buildings for other uses, the most notable is a plan to turn the site into a movie and television studio. The current plan, set to begin soon, is to build housing and commercial structures along the waterfront, which boasts some of the best views available of the Narrows and Manhattan. (David Goldfarb collection.)

Visit us at
arcadiapublishing.com